How to Find a Network Marketing Goldmine

Researching and Evaluating MLM Opportunities

By

Praveen Kumar & Prashant Kumar

Terms of Use

Disclaimer

The advice contained in this material might not be suitable for everyone. The author obtained the information from sources believed to be reliable and from his own personal experience, but he neither implies nor intends any guarantee of accuracy.

The author, publisher and distributors never give legal, accounting, medical or any other type of professional advice. The reader must always seek those services from competent professionals that can review their own circumstances.

The author, publisher and distributors particularly disclaim any liability, loss, or risk taken by individuals who directly or indirectly act on the information contained herein. All readers must accept full responsibility for their use of this material.

All pictures used in this book are for illustrative purposes only. The people in the pictures are not connected with the book, author or publisher and no link or endorsement between any of them and the topic or content is implied, nor should any be assumed. The pictures are only licensed for use in

Table of Contents

Chapter 1: Introduction

It is likely that you are reading this book because you are seriously interested in joining a network marketing opportunity. You may have been approached by trusted friends and family members and are so excited by the opportunity that you just want to jump right in. I am here to tell you to slow down and really evaluate things properly. Do not be swayed by slick presentations no matter who they are from. The opportunity may be exciting and network marketing itself is exciting for reasons explained below, but is the opportunity you are looking at right for you as an individual? Have you properly assessed all the variables such as if the industry segment is right for you, if the company is legitimate, what their marketing plan is and who their management team is? These are just some of the things you really need to investigate before signing anything. Adequate research is critical to your success for many reasons. The most obvious reasons are as follows:

1. You don't want to rush to join a company and invest your time, money and hard work, only for the company to go under

because the product became obsolete or was a fad product.

2. You don't want to join a company which on the surface seems good but underneath all the hype is making a loss because eventually, that loss will pass down to you.

3. You don't want to risk your credibility by joining a company which is not legitimate.

4. You want to join under a sponsor and be on a team which is supportive and wants you to succeed.

These are just some of the reasons why it is so important to research which company you go with. Most people join network marketing companies in a rush because of flashy, exciting presentations without really thinking it through and then wonder why they ended up jumping around from company to company. This is counterproductive and this book will allow you to be focused in your efforts so that you end up choosing the best opportunity for yourself as an individual. There is no such thing as a perfect company, but there is such a perfect company for YOU. By evaluating your network marketing opportunities according to the principles in this book, you will be able to uncover your very own network marketing goldmine.

Why is Network Marketing Exciting?

Network marketing represents a unique opportunity to set yourself up in business from home. The cost of setting up as a network marketer is relatively little (on average $100 USD) compared to what you would expect to pay if you wanted to set yourself up in business from scratch. Aside from that, you can generate unlimited earnings from your downline. Once you establish a good team, there is a potential for residual earnings for as long as you decide to stay as a member of that team. More importantly, even if you decide to stop working in the future, you can continue to earn a residual income from your downline. If that is not exciting, I don't know what is!

The History of Network Marketing

The first ever documented network marketing plan was put in place and executed successfully by a health product company called Nutrilite in 1945. The system was set up to motivate sales people to go the extra mile to make sales for the company. Health products like vitamins were sold to sales people at a 35% discount. On top of that, the company paid a 25% bonus on top of any profit made every month. Sales people were encouraged to sell more by the prospect of becoming a direct distributor. Basically, each salesperson had to find 25 customers, after which point, they were promoted as direct distributors, which essentially meant that they could hire their own sales teams and train them to sell products. To encourage direct distributors to train their staff very well, the company offered a 2% commission on total sales once the team had managed to find 150 customers. Their downline went only one level deep, but you can see the potential that this model offered.

Network Marketing Size and Potential

Just to give you an idea of the potential for network marketing, in 1949, Rich DeVos and Jay Van Andel joined Nutrilite as distributors. They had a disagreement with the company and left to go and set up the company Amway. Amway was formed in 1959 and in 1972, it was so successful using network marketing, that it could acquire Nutrilite and incorporate its products into its own product portfolio. Amway is now one of the biggest network marketing companies in history with reported 2011 revenues being a massive

$10.9 billion. In 2010, Forbes ranked Amway as the 32nd largest privately-held company in the USA and Deloitte ranked it as the 114th largest privately-held company in the world.

One of the most respected names in the world of network marketing is Leonard Clements. He is the founder of Marketwave, a highly regarded watchdog organization. Clements likes to play the devil's advocate when it comes to network marketing and tends to call things exactly as they are. According to Clement, there are several factors that could make network marketing an explosion on its way. The biggest of these factors is the current economic situation. The network marketing industry had one of its biggest boom periods during the recession of the early 90's. History has shown us that when people find it difficult to find jobs, they turn to alternative solutions like network marketing. The explosion of the internet and social networking also makes network

marketing a much more attractive prospect for people who assume they have to sell to friends and family. The new dawn of social media means that you can easily set up networks and teams all over the world without even having to leave your house.

The Direct Selling Association is a national trade association for companies who engage in direct sales. Currently there are 200 members of the organisation including some pretty major names. In the 90's, the proportion of member companies who engaged in network marketing was just 25 per cent. In 2009, that figure was closer to 99.6 per cent. It is estimated that there are currently over 1000 US companies who engage in network marketing and that figure is growing exponentially. In addition, Direct Selling Association statistics state that the number of people engaging in network marketing as a business is around 56 million which equates to around two million people per country! Network marketing statistics from January 2012 show sales of more than 100 billion US dollars worldwide. In the last ten years, the industry has grown 90 per cent. Very few industries can compare to this level of growth. The only way to explain this massive growth is that increasing numbers of people are becoming tired of the nine to five jobs and are in their search to find something which could free them from that, and have found network marketing.

The Importance of Investigating Opportunities

There are many companies jumping on the network marketing bandwagon with slick presentations and sales letters to draw you in. Some companies may be audacious enough to tell you that they are the best networking marketing company to work for. One thing that you should know without doubt before proceeding is that there is no such thing as a perfect network marketing opportunity. There is no best company to work for. You can however, do a little bit of research choose the best network marketing company for you. Before committing your precious time and money to any network marketing opportunity, it is critical that you properly evaluate the proposition you are faced with. One of the leading management consulting firms to network marketing businesses in the world is a company called the Wood International Group. With more than thirty years of experience in the industry, they know what they are talking about. According to them, investigating the claims of the company you are going to work for is critical to your future success. In addition, it is likely that to start off, you will be introducing the opportunity to your family, friends and associates and as such, you want to ensure that your credibility remains intact!

There are many legitimate companies out there and in fact, network marketing has emerged from controversy as a perfectly legitimate profession, the same way as franchising. However, legislation and big successful companies can't fully stop occasional bad apples from finding their way into the fruit basket! There are companies out there who will entice you with glossy sales presentations, making all sorts of false claims about how much money you can make by joining them and by recruiting your own team. Companies like these are usually promoting pyramid schemes which are illegal in some countries and will only result in you wasting your time, money and energy on nothing but false promises. The usual scenario is that the people giving the presentations to you are the only ones who are making money, not the people listening to the presentations. They are usually the ones who hand over their money blindly, only to discover later that they have been ripped-off. It is because of these so- called bad apples, that the industry has become a closely-scrutinized one, especially in the United States. The USA government has some legislation which helps to weed out the bad apples and generally, these rules can be applied no matter where you are in the world, to help you personally to identify a good network marketing company to invest in.

What This Book Is All About

We will go exactly how you can investigate a company later in this book and how to decide what type of company to go for. The company you choose should reflect what you are passionate about, what your interests are and your field of expertise. Obviously, some training and learning is to be expected, but never forget the adage that enthusiasm sells! You cannot be enthused about something you have no interest in. There are many other things to consider when choosing your network marketing company, including the management team, their financial situation, the products, the compensation scheme, code of ethics and their company culture. These things help you identify if you are a good fit for the company. After all, you could potentially spend years of your life working with them to build a residual income. The quality and marketability of the products is also an important thing to look at and will be discussed at length. The aim of this book is ultimately to equip you with all the tools and knowledge required to choose a network marketing company which not only allows you to build residual income, but also suits who you are as an individual, allowing you to stay with them and build a residual income for many years to come.

Chapter 2: Researching the Network Marketing Industry

When choosing the company that you want to join, making the wrong choice due to improper research can be a very expensive mistake to make. Expensive not just in terms of potential lost income and the cost of investing, but also expensive in terms of lost credibility among your family, friends and associates. The three major components of network marketing are: the industry itself, the way that the company you join is structured and the activities of the distributors within the company.

In your evaluation, if you understand these three things, you will be closer to making the best decision for you.

The network marketing industry can be thought of in the following way:

1. Network marketing companies.

2. Network marketing company suppliers.

3. Network marketing associations.

4. Network marketing distributors or representatives.

For the purposes of deciding on which company to join, an in depth understanding of the industry is not necessary. However, it is helpful to know about the companies within the industry, the way it is subdivided and which product types or industry segments within the network marketing industry have the most potential. This is discussed below.

Which industries are the most successful and why?

According to MLM training giant Nexera, there are 25 network marketing companies in the world, 22 are health and wellness companies, two are technology companies and only one is a service company.

In network marketing, history shows that the most successful companies produce consumable products. What I mean by consumable is products which can be used up in a relatively short space of time and replaced. If you establish a good and loyal customer base, it is then possible to see how growing the business can lead to sustainable residual income in the long term which keeps paying you even if you stop trying to grow the business. Non- consumable products such as computers, lap tops and other technological items are usually one-off sales because they tend to be expensive items which do not require regular replacement. Consumable products are ideal for the network marketing business model.

Taking a closer look at the top 25 lists, the two technology companies are ACN and 5Linx, which are both telecommunications companies. Looking at their products, they sell consumable technology. Technology which needs to be paid for on a regular basis. For example, 5Linx sells video phone and VOIP (voice over internet protocol) services, as well as data centre services, a tablet computer, text messaging services, energy services, internet services, cell phones and plans, credit card services, security systems and satellite television. Aside from the tablet computer, every one of the services they provide requires regular payments. Some may even require customers to sign up to minimum term contracts. Therefore, this company is one of the most successful network marketing companies in existence, and one of only two technology companies at the top of the list.

ACN, much like 5Linx, also sells consumable technology in the form of energy, phone services, internet services, television services, home security and technical support. Again, all consumable technology is those where people must sign up to and pay for monthly. Technology companies must keep their list of products diverse because technology moves at an astounding rate and there is always the risk where new technology will become obsolete in a couple of years.

The only service company on the list is Legalshield. Legalshield acts almost like an insurance company where clients pay a monthly subscription fee and are covered for any legal assistance they may need at any point during their membership. Again, the company is successful because it gets regular payments from its customers.

The common denominator with all the network marketing companies included in the top 25 lists is that they sell consumable products which either requires regular replacement, or which require regular payments from their customers. All companies on the list have been in existence for a minimum of 10 years. This does not mean that they are safe, or that signing up with a start-up is a mistake, it is just something to consider when you make your decision. Are you a risk taker or do you like to play things safe?

There is a distinct lack of industry statistics regarding the profitability of individual sectors within the network marketing industry, but just to give you an idea, the largest and most profitable network marketing company globally at the time of writing is Amway. Current figures show estimated revenue of 10.9 billion US dollars. 5Linx is privately owned, so their financial data are not for public record, however, they were ranked on the Rochester list of 100 fastest growing companies in 2011. ACN, the only other telecommunications company on the top 25 list reported profits of 50 million US dollars in 2010. Lastly, Legalshield reported profits of 472 million US dollars in 2011.

There are a whole host of other factors which you need to consider before deciding which company to go for, but it is a good idea to start with the industry sector that you are interested in. These are not the only industry sectors covered by network marketing companies, but they are the most successful. Once you know what industry sector you are most interested in, start researching individual companies within that industry. Remember, bigger does not necessarily mean better. Better is what is best for you!

Chapter 3: How to Evaluate Companies within an Industry

Once you have identified the industry you want to work within, the next task is to find the best company within that industry to work with. There have been difficulties over the years, however, network marketing has emerged as a legitimate business and as such, depending on where you are in the world, and there are regulations which need to be adhered to. In the USA, federal and state governments aid the network marketing industry and as such, the non-legitimate companies are easier to identify. Differentiating illegal pyramid schemes from legitimate network marketing opportunities is of paramount importance, even though awareness of them is such that they are being eradicated over time.

In the USA, it is prohibited for a company to remunerate sales people for the sole purpose of recruiting others into the company. In addition, companies must sell sales kits to the sales representatives at cost price. At the most basic level, it is essential that you find out how the company operates, especially if you do not live in a country like USA where network marketing companies are so closely regulated. Simply by asking them if they pay for recruiting sales people and if they sell their sales materials at cost price to sales people, you can get an idea of their legitimacy. Any company that places more emphasis on recruiting other sales people than selling products is highly likely to be a bad apple. Just to give you an example, Amway makes it very clear on their website that it is illegal in the United States for an affiliate to convince another person to make payment to them or the company in exchange for getting benefits for convincing people to accept the opportunity. The website states that one should not allow individuals to mislead others into thinking that they can earn ridiculously high income from network marketing, as such claims are likely to be false. They put this on their website as a warning.

It is a warning which should be heeded with respect to any company you are investigating. Always ask questions about signing people up and ask them to back up any claims they make about ridiculous sounding income claims. Find out the following information to determine just how legitimate they are.

- -Are they real products, or are they simply selling a façade to cover up a pyramid scheme?

- -Does the company engage in the practice of inventory loading? Inventory loading is the act of forcing distributors to purchase large amounts of stock to meet targets. This practice is unethical. Do not join a company who does this or, do so at your own risk!

- -Is purchasing additional accessories and products a mandatory requirement for distributors? If so, then steer clear.

- -Overly inflated representations of potential earnings. Things that are too good to be true usually are not.

There are several other things that it is prudent to know before entering business with a company. It is a lot easier to discover these things than you may think.

Profitability and Reputability

Whether or not you can access information regarding a company's profitability depends on their status. If the companies you are looking at are public companies, they are obliged to reveal their financial information to the public. You can easily get their financial information by doing a quick search on Forbes, Google Finance or Yahoo Finance. If you live in the UK, or the company is based in the UK, you can find the information at Companies House, which is an executive branch of the government and it is the official registrar of companies. Once you have the information, simply go to the 'profit and loss' accounts to find out what the company's net profit is. Net profit is Gross profit less all expenses, so the figure will give you an idea as to how profitable the company is. Amway is an example of a highly-profitable company and their earnings disclosure statement is freely available on their website.

If, on the other hand the company is privately-held, the company is under no obligation to release its financial statements to the public; however, because you could be a potential investor, you are well within your rights to ask them about their profitability.

An organisation called Direct Selling Association (DSA) can be thought of as a trade organisation set up to regulate companies that engage in direct selling. More than 99 percent of companies registered with them are in the network marketing business. The DSA in the United States is affiliated with the National Retail Federation and any company who is a member pledges to abide by its code of ethics. The DSA has sister organisations in other countries including the UK, Australia, Malaysia, New Zealand and Singapore. While being included to the DSA does not guarantee the reputability of a company, it is a good place to start.

In addition, if you are in USA, Canada or UK, find out if the company you are eyeing is in good standing with the Better Business Bureau (BBB). The BBB has been established since 1912 and is an unbiased organisation which sets and upholds high standards for company behaviour. Belonging to the BBB is a marker of credibility itself. The BBB take claims of bad business practices very seriously and may revoke membership if investigations prove allegations to be true. Obviously, nothing is absolute and even the best companies have complaints against them. You can find out just how well they handle complaints from the BBB and this information can be vital to your decision-making process.

Below is a short check-list to help you to discover how reputable a company is:

— Are they with the DSA?

- Are they in good standing with the BBB? Check out their standing with the Attorney General and the Chamber of Commerce as well. A lack of complaint is no guarantee of a company's legitimacy.

- How long have they been in business? More than 10 years is exceptional in the world of network marketing, however, all companies were once start-ups, so look at the other criteria if they are a relatively new.

- Is a comprehensive training course provided?

- Is there a non-negotiable monthly fee for membership?

- Is there a minimum quota for sales before you will be paid?

- Do the costs allow you to be profitable?

- What is their compensation structure? Will the structure allow you to be profitable in the short, medium and long term?

Although not particularly scientific, online rating sites can give you an idea about how reputable a company is. Again, nothing is absolute and many companies engage in paying writers to write good reviews about them. Please note that most companies have some people who have had bad experiences, so there may be one or two complaints; however, if most of ratings are good and all other criteria are satisfied, the company is likely to be credible.

-What is the general buzz about the company and its products on websites and blogs?

-What newspaper and magazine stories can you find on them? A simple Google search can reveal a lot but remember to check through several pages of the results to get the maximum amount of information about them.

Who Owns The Company?

Knowing about the company's owners and management team is essential. A credible team at the top can be the difference between a company failing, and a company doing spectacularly well. With a little bit of research, it is relatively easy to find out who owns any company. A quick Google search or a look at the company's website should reveal this information. Once you find out who the owners are, put your Colombo hat on and do a bit of background digging to find out if they are trustworthy and what their reputation is. Find out if their background makes them credible as business owners in your niche. Most company websites display biographies of their owners. In addition, Google search can reveal a lot of information. The BBB also holds information on the past business performance of its member company's owners. Check with them to find out how credible company owners are.

Knowing The Company's Philosophy

If you ever worked for a corporate institution at any level, it is highly likely that you have heard the term "company philosophy" used. Many managers use it without explaining what that philosophy is. Essentially, it is a set of rules which are often established over time through trial, error and leadership which govern how things are done and how a company's staff are expected to behave. Company philosophies often include rules regarding how decisions are made, company ethics and how people are treated and judged. Knowing the company philosophy is important because if the philosophy is not aligned with your own philosophy, you may not be a good fit for the company. For example, if you are a staunch environmentalist and the company you are investigating is being hounded by Greenpeace for polluting the environment with its dodgy practices, you are highly unlikely to feel comfortable working for them. This is an extreme example, but it illustrates the point. Most companies have a statement about their company philosophy on their website. You can also get a good feel for how a company operates by simply speaking with people who work for them.

Knowing The Company's Track Record

Knowing the company's past track record for sales is somewhat an indicator of future success. However, keep in mind that even a good track record showing consistent growth year after year is no guarantee of future success. Sudden bad news or economic changes can affect even the largest and most successful companies. A company with a good track record of sales is one which grows its net profit (profit after tax) year after year. You can find this information by requesting the disclosure documents from the registrar of companies in the country. All public companies have to file these documents with the registrar of companies every year. Some privately held companies will release their disclosure documents on request and often for a fee. The disclosure documents will also provide information on the management team and the owners. You will often be able to find pertinent information about their track record and even their salary in the disclosure documents.

Is The Company Privately-Owned Or Publicly-Listed?

A publicly-held company, also known as a public-limited company in the UK, is a company which offers its stock for sale on the stock market or in similar open markets to the public. What this means is that large amounts of capital can be raised relatively quickly by issuing shares to the public and the owners of the shares benefit from earning money in the form of dividends from the securities they purchased. Because the shares are available to the public, publicly-listed companies are required by law to disclose their financial statements and they tend to have many shareholders. Privately-listed companies on the other hand, are owned privately and their shares are not available for purchase by the public. This does not mean that they do not have shareholders, on the contrary, most do, but typically, they have fewer shareholders than publicly-listed companies.

Public Company Advantages

– Can raise large amounts of capital quickly.

- You can easily access their financial statements as they are in the public domain.

Disadvantages

- Bureaucracy! Sometimes management teams in publicly-held companies can get so caught up with corporate governance and reporting, hence the focus is shifted away from the operations and growth.

Privately-Held Company Advantages

- Because they do not have to disclose financial information, they can sometimes have a competitive advantage compared to a publicly-held company in the same position.

- Because they do not have to deal with corporate governance and reporting, management can often focus more on growth and day-to-day operations.

Privately-Held Disadvantages

-You cannot access their financial records easily, meaning you must make your decision based on factors that do not include profitability unless they disclose them on request.

Chapter 4: Evaluating Companies Management Team

It is just as important for a company to have a good management team as it is for them to have reputable owners and directors. To find the members of the management team is not difficult. Most companies have some information on their management teams clearly displayed on their website. Failing that, the company brochure and prospectus is likely to have lots of information about the management teams. Someone interested in becoming a distributor can easily request a company brochure or prospectus by phone or email. Once you have the names of the people on the management team, it is possible with a little research to find out just how good they are. This chapter will deal with how to recognise a good management team, the importance of knowing their track record and getting to know the management teams.

How To Recognize A Good Management Team

Strong leadership is essential if a company wants to be successful. Good network marketing management teams stay up-to-date with the latest news on marketing and promotion. In addition, they are constantly involved with the business and communicate continuously with their teams.

Good management requires a wide range of skills including, but not limited to leadership, planning, delegation and excellent communication skills. Good managers take their cues from the top and are responsible for effectively communicating the vision of the company to the team and for delegating tasks which are purposely designed to fulfil those requirements. Being good at delegation is essential as it is important to know the unique skills of each person within the team and to delegate tasks appropriately for the highest level of efficiency. Of course, of utmost importance is motivation. Any good management team in a network marketing company will be experts at motivating people using various techniques.

Communication is very important and the ability to communicate effectively with different people is a must in any industry, especially as a manager. Again, enthusiasm sells, so any good management team will have an infectious passion for what they are doing which is easy to recognise. Being progressive and able to take constructive criticism is another sign of good management. In addition, planning and setting objectives and setting a good reward structure are essential components which help to motivate team members. Different people react in different ways to different situations. What I mean by this is that your unique personality will dictate what management style best suits you. Ask questions specifically tailored to find out about a company's management style. This will help you to assess first if they have a good management team, and second, if that management team is in tune with your personality and style of working.

Commitment to Quality, Employees and Ethics

The commitment of the leadership to quality will be evident in everything they do and the answers to the questions below will tell you a lot.

1. Who are the leaders?

2. What is their background?

3. How did they get into network marketing?

4. What did they do before they became involved in network marketing?

5. Can you talk to the leaders at events?

6. Are they regularly available on training calls and webinars?

7. Are they just a figurehead, a face for the company newsletter?

8. How involved are they in the business?

Does the management team act with integrity always? The definition of integrity is essentially the adherence to moral principles and ethics always. Integrity is difficult to judge if you do not know somebody well or do not have access to a lot of information about them. However, the level of transparency regarding company profits, company ethics, the company business plan, their mission statement and their goals for the future will tell you an awful lot. If this information is readily available via the company website or in a company prospectus, it is likely that the management team adheres to ethical standards. If not, you may want to take a closer look or skip them altogether.

These things are important to know as the leadership of a company is the future of the company and ultimately your future, should you decide to join them.

Getting to Know the Management Team

Getting to know your potential management team is not as difficult as it sounds and is an important element of deciding upon whether to sign up to the company or not. Below are some key things you need to find out to get to know your management team:

1. What did they do before they joined the company? What were their responsibilities? Knowing these will give you an idea as to what they can or cannot handle.

2. How did they come to be in that position? Did someone lose their job prompting a promotion or were they promoted from within? Are they from outside the company to sort out some issues or not? Knowing this information will help you to understand what people within the company think of the management team.

3. What are plans they have for the future of the company? What aspirations do they have for themselves? The last question may be more difficult to find out unless you can talk to them directly.

4. How does the management team fit in with the larger structure of the company? This is something your potential sponsor should be able to tell you.

5. What kind of relationship does the management team have with their superiors, if there are any people above them?

6. Are the management team the kind of people to stand for their subordinates? Are they actively involved in company politics? Do they stick their necks out for their distributors if something bad happens?

7. What kind of management style do they have? Do they get actively involved and keep up with the day-to-day operations of the business or are they just watching things done from a distance?

8. Do they micromanage every little detail or do they stand back and give you enough rope to hang yourself? Maybe something in between?

9. Find out a little something about their personal lives if possible. Religious beliefs, political stance, hobbies, children, spouses. These things could have an impact on the amount of time they dedicate to the company and therefore on you as a distributor.

There is a theory that the more you know about those above you in any kind of company, the better chance you have of getting on well within that company. Take time to do a little bit of investigative work. It will pay off in the long run.

Chapter 5: How to Evaluate a Company's Products and Services?

The product you sell is the foundation upon which your future success will be built in any network marketing firm. For this reason, it is imperative that you fully evaluate the product that you may end up selling. A good network marketing company is built around a robust product line that has an appeal to the target market which is sustainable over time. Any company built around shoddy products with slick, over-hyped compensation plans should be avoided at all costs. This chapter will lay out some simple things to evaluate network marketing companies' products.

Quality Of Products

The company should sell products of superior quality and the price should reflect that quality. Any product which can easily be bought in the supermarket for a similar or lesser price is not worth investing and should be avoided. Network marketing products should be made from superior materials or ingredients, things that are not available to every Tom, Dick or Harry in the supermarket. Most companies will describe their products in their product description. Do a bit of research and find out if their claims are true before investing.

Are The Products Consumable? Are They Unique?

The products should be innovative and have a broad appeal. Products which are fads should be avoided, unless you want to get in, make a quick buck and get out. Faddy products tend to sell very well in the initial launch phase and tend to lose their appeal when consumers realise they have gone out of fashion. An example of a faddy product is the dryer balls a few years ago. When they were first launched, there was a lot of hype around them with television commercials and sales people making all sorts of claims. The main selling point is that, they were so effective, that they shortened dryer times and made all your clothes fluffy and soft, reducing the need for fabric softener. That company did not last very long and to this day, most people probably could not even remember the name of the company. Save your time, money and credibility and avoid fad products if you can. Look for products with lasting appeal which are more likely to survive in the long term and bring you a residual income for many years to come. Find out what other similar products are in the market and what market share your company has. Products which have a broad appeal to a large customer-based are more likely to be successful in the long run. Examples of this include nutritional products and those used at home.

Life Cycle Of The Product

Work out if the product is relevant to the marketplace or not. Assuming you are into selling products which you have some knowledge and passion of, you should have some idea of what is going on in the marketplace and how relevant the network marketing products are in the market. Aside from your gut instinct and knowing what is going on in the marketplace regarding the particular product you are looking at, your research should give you some idea of how fast the company is actually growing year over year. For example, if the company is growing at a rate of 10 percent year over year, you should expect your efforts in the field to reflect that.

It is difficult to tell just how long a new product will last in the marketplace. New and innovative technologies come and go all the time as the rate of innovation in today's technology-driven world means that things are constantly moving on. Unless you are prepared to get in and ride on the wave of some new technology, get the money and get out, it might be best to keep things simple. Consumable products allow you to generate repeat business from your customers. By building a wide customer base, it is entirely possible to build a substantial residual income over time.

Consumable products include skin care products, nutritional products, and other personal care products. The residual income potential for non-consumable products such as electrical items is not as high compared to the consumable products because customers are more likely to only buy the product once. It is possible to make money but you will likely need to get a lot of referrals from existing customers and constantly must look for new customers in order to build your income.

There are some technological products which are considered consumable simply because they require monthly payments. 5Linx and ACN are the only two companies in the top 25 network marketing companies that are produced by industry giant Nexera. As discussed in the chapter on evaluating network marketing industries, these two companies sell telecommunications services, satellite TV services, credit card services and a whole host of other technology-based services which all require monthly payment plans and sometimes customers are required to sign contracts for a fixed term. If you are interested in technology, it is sensible to pick a company like this which sells a variety of consumable technological services so that you can build a long-term residual income.

MLM Companies And Bankruptcy

With that being said, this does not mean that network marketing companies which sell consumables cannot get into trouble. The company Arbonne was declared bankrupt in 2010 despite selling superior skin care and personal care products (which reportedly produce visible results very quickly). While distributors were happy with the company, many reported that some of their products lasted so long, (sometimes six months), therefore made repeat orders slow. Unless they had a wide customer base or a huge downline, it was very difficult for them to build a significant referral income because the rate of repeat orders was low. In addition, the company had a mandatory minimum order of $100 a month for its distributors, which some complained was a financial burden when they were not making enough sales to cover the costs. Their marketing plan was also structured around doing home parties which are time consuming and difficult to sell at. While these things are unlikely to be the main reason for bankruptcy, it made it challenging for their distributors. All these factors should be taken into consideration when evaluating the products of your potential network marketing company.

A network marketing company called Dynamic Essentials, based in Florida, used to be a distributor of a seaweed extract called Royal Tongan Limu. The extract wa marketed as a new health supplement and the company made wild claims about the product which were illegal. As a result, they found themselves in trouble with the Food and Drug Administration (FDA) and were forced to close leaving a lot of disillusioned distributors behind. This is an example of a potentially fad like product which got people excited about unrealistic health benefits. When it comes to anything that humans can consume, it is important to do some fact checking and ensure that the product is approved by the FDA or its equivalent in your country.

Sunshine Empire was a network marketing company set up in 2006 in Singapore. The company reportedly sold investment schemes and managed to collect $189 million from unsuspecting investors via its distributors. Investigations later revealed that the company was in fact an illegal Ponzi scheme and the company was subsequently closed. Any company selling what appears to be an investment scheme via multi-level marketing may be a scam like this. Either steer clear, or thoroughly investigate the legitimacy of the company and its owners. This example is a clear indication as to why the safest bet for network marketing is usually a company which sells actual physical products.

Marketability Issues

Marketing is the cornerstone of any network marketing business! You may have the highest quality product in the world, but if you do not have a good marketing strategy, and your price is not pitched correctly, you will make little or no money!

In some network marketing companies, the only people who buy their products are their own representatives! Sounds ridiculous, but it is true. This is because the public do not believe that there is value in the product and the only people who perceive the real value of the product are the representatives themselves. The reason is because the value they see is in the opportunity that the product represents. Making money from other distributors! Clearly, this is not a sustainable business model and most distributors will give up quickly. You need to ensure that the marketing strategy is unique enough to get people to buy the product you are selling without having to join the business. The question you need to ask yourself when evaluating the products of a company is:

"If the company was not offering this network marketing opportunity, would people still buy the products?"

The important thing is that the marketing strategy needs to be unique enough so that people who are not a part of the business see a reason to buy it. There must be a perception of value to the potential customer. It could be something as simple as buy one and get one free, or get your friend to buy one and get yours free WITHOUT having to join the business. A good marketing strategy combined with a superior product that people want to buy is a recipe for success.

Also, ask yourself if you are interested in the products. Would you buy them? Ask for samples and try them yourself. If you like them and are genuinely excited about them, they will be easy to sell.

What To Sell

As an individual, there will be things that you will undoubtedly be naturally drawn to and feel passionate about. In addition, there may be products which you may have some knowledge about. For obvious reasons, it is more likely that you will be able to sell something you already feel passionate about, have an interest in and are knowledgeable about, than something which bores you to tears! Think for a second... Are you naturally passionate and knowledgeable about beauty products? Or do you naturally lean more towards health and nutrition? Are you a bit of a technology geek? Can you see where I am going with this? There is a whole host of network marketing companies out there selling everything you can imagine! Search for one which sells quality products that are in line with your passions. After training and getting all the marketing materials, not only will you become an expert, but you will also turn into a happier expert who is passionate and excited about what you are selling. What do you get if you put passion, enthusiasm, knowledge, marketability and a good product all in the head of a network marketer? A recipe for success!

Product Training

A good network marketing company will offer a good amount of training and standard support as well as good quality marketing materials. You should not have to pay extortionate fees for training and marketing materials. We will look at product training in a bit more depth later in chapter six.

Product Delivery

It is important to be aware of things like product delivery and cost, particularly if it is likely to be a bulky product as you may encounter storage issues in your home. Some companies require you to buy a minimum amount of stock every month. If this is the case, find out how much the minimum order is and if it is a viable amount for you to handle if your sales dip for a month or two. You should never buy what you cannot sell, but you will only know what you can sell once you start selling! Find out if the company will purchase back unsold stocks from you.

Does The Company Sell Exclusively Through Affiliates?

This is an important question to ask and something which can seriously affect your potential sales results. Clearly if the company sells directly to the market through a website, the company might compete against you for sales in your area. There are companies who sell their products through retailers and in Amazon. This is unethical and directly conflicts with the products that affiliates are trying to sell. You should avoid joining companies that compete directly with their affiliates in the marketplace.

Beware also of using affiliate links to get people buy online. These typically have the company website with your affiliate id attached at the end in a very long URL. It is so easy for your lead to just go directly to the website instead of your affiliate id and buy the product. This means that you miss out the commission you worked so hard to get. Many companies use technology which means you will never miss out commissions this way. Ask the question and qualify the answer to be on the safe side.

The Compensation Plan

The compensation plan will dictate how much money you can make, so it is essential that you understand and evaluate it well. The complexity of compensation plans can be a bit daunting though, which makes comparison of plans a little difficult. If there is anything you do not understand about a plan you are evaluating, ask! You need to work out how realistic their claims are. Below are a few factors to consider when evaluating a company's compensation plan:

- How many new distributors will you have to sign up before being eligible for compensation?

- What is the minimum amount of cash sales you need to generate before being eligible for compensation?

- What is the difference in earning potential between recruiting new distributors and selling products?

- Are non-monetary rewards and cash bonuses included in the compensation plan?

Apart from being an important consideration for you personally, the compensation plan is much more important to anyone of your future downline. Even if you decide to stick it out with a company which does not provide the best compensation plan, other distributors in your downline may leave, losing you money. The compensation plan is important not only for you in making the decision, but also in terms of retaining potential future distributors in your team. Evaluate it very carefully and compare the plans of several companies that you are interested in.

Chapter 6: Training Provided by the Company

Importance Of A Good Training Program

We mentioned briefly in the last section that a good training program is essential in any network marketing company. A good training program with additional training materials is essential. Training programs significantly reduce the amount of work you have to do by yourself.

When you sign up as a new distributor for a network marketing company, you typically sign up under a sponsor. Your sponsor is usually the person who introduced you to the business in the first place and in many cases, they are responsible with much of your training. Finding out what kind of support you will get from your sponsor is critical to your success as a distributor. Obviously, how good your sponsor is will depend for the most part on what kind of person they are and training materials they are provided by the company. Some sponsors are responsible and helpful and will guide you on the right path so that you are successful. After all, your success means their success since they typically earn commission from what you sell. Such sponsors may provide you with leads as well as helping you with your marketing. However, some sponsors will leave you dangling in the wind by yourself without any support which is not helpful to you. Whoever your sponsor is, if you plan on staying in the business for a long term, it is likely that you will be working with them for a long time, so make sure that they are suitable and that you like them by asking the right questions.

Evaluating Training

The training package ultimately depends on the company. In some companies, your sponsor will be responsible in organising training events and workshops. In some cases, you may have to pay a small fee for extra training, but this should not be an extortionate amount of money. Find out exactly what kind of support and training is offered and what it's frequency is. Also find out how long the initial training lasts and about ongoing training throughout your time at the company. Training should not just stop after the initial training. As new products are launched and new marketing strategies implemented, it is important to keep all distributors up to date.

Look for the following in the distributor package:

- Will the company train you or help you with regard to acquiring new leads?

- Do they offer training in the form of 'in person' or 'online' coaching sessions?

- Do they offer training DVD's to keep at home?

- Do they have quality and up-to-date marketing materials as a part of the package?

- Do they have quality marketing presentations on DVD?

- Do they offer webinars and training workshops?

- Do they offer teleconference training sessions?

- Is there a fee for product and marketing training?

- How much does product and marketing training cost?

- Will you be training with your team at regular coaching sessions and meetings?

Chapter 7: Marketing Material and Support

All network marketing companies should provide marketing materials as a standard practice. Of course, the quality of the materials may vary between companies. Marketing materials and marketing support usually come from your sponsor.

What Marketing Materials Are Provided?

Find out what kind of marketing materials are provided by the company. For example:

- Do they provide DVD presentations?

- Do they provide presentation flip charts?

- Do they provide customer leaflets and brochures?

The company may provide slick marketing materials; however, the information contained in the marketing materials is critical to how effective you will be at selling. Therefore marketing materials are sometimes referred to as sales aids. Look for the following in all marketing materials:

-The company should clearly lay out all the features of the product and the benefits to the customer should be heavily stressed.

-They should have third party endorsement to back up any claims that they make with regards to the benefits of the product. Look for endorsement in the form of newspaper articles, and independent studies to ensure credibility of the claims.

What Is The Cost Of The Marketing Materials?

Ask your potential sponsor about the marketing materials. Some companies require you to pay for marketing materials and others do not. The cost can be very high. Part of your evaluation should be whether or not you can actually afford the marketing materials and how often you would be expected to purchase them. If the materials are ridiculously expensive, it will be obvious that the company is making money from selling marketing materials to its distributors. If this is the case, how likely is it that they are selling volumes of their product? The product is where they should be making their money, not their marketing materials. There have been horror stories of companies claiming that their representatives did not have to buy their expensive marketing materials, but who then went on to treat the same representatives with disdain if they did not! Steer clear of such companies. If you are not sure, ask for the contact details of other distributors and ask all of them the same questions.

Does The Company Allow Internet Marketing?

Social media has become so integrated into the lives of people all around the world, that most companies use social media marketing to effectively target their customer base and grow their sales. The thing about social media is that so many people sit on their accounts passively and actively that they are fast becoming consumer recommendation machines as well as a place to network and share. People trust their friends and relatives more than they trust slick advertising campaigns, which is only natural. Any business which implements an effective social media campaign will reap the benefits in the long run of personal recommendations and often, a viral spread of their brand over the internet. Gone are the days when cold calling is a must in selling products. Internet is a means that makes promotion much easier for those who despise the idea of cold calling. Blogs and social media channels that point back to a dedicated website from which you can sell your product are so important to your success in this technology-driven age. Find out from your sponsor if social media marketing is allowed and how you can integrate it with your own personal marketing strategy. Some companies may even have websites already integrated with social media which then become your affiliate website. You can create your branded social media channels to help with your promotional activities. The internet is an extremely important part of any business marketing strategy. Ensure that your network marketing company is keeping up with the times so that your income potential is maximized.

With that being said, not everyone is comfortable with Facebook, Twitter, search engine optimization and blogging. Some people prefer the offline approach to marketing. While in today's environment, this might mean that a significant amount of money is left on the table; this should not mean that internet marketing is compulsory. Any good network marketing company will have options for both online and offline marketing with adequate support provided based on individual preference.

Company Support

In addition to the training program, how the company supports its representatives speaks volumes about the company. Sales people are the backbone of any company so it should treat their sales people accordingly. Most companies publish details of their support systems via their websites. Look for the following information:

- What is the system for addressing issues?

- Can you contact a company representative by phone or email easily?

- Do they respond readily?

This is important because you do not want a company which places all of the responsibility on your sponsor to resolve issues. If the support system is weak, and by support, I mean training and marketing materials as well as distributor support in case something goes wrong, then it can put a lot of undue pressure on your sponsor. A stressed-out sponsor is unlikely to be able to provide the support that you need. Again, speak to other distributors and ask questions. If you find the answers vague, follow-up with questions to get clarity until you are 100 percent sure of what they are saying about the company. It is important to know that some companies pay their distributors to give decoy answers so that enquiring minds are convinced that all is well within the company. Beware of this!

Marketing System and Sales Funnel Support

Any good network marketing company should have an appropriate system in dealing with leads once you have them. Whether the leads are captured online or offline, there should be a support system in place to help you to organize your leads and customers. Ask the following questions to be sure:

- Is there a process in place for you to gather the contact information of leads easily and quickly? This could be a diary system offline or an online form.

- Is there a system in place to deal with the leads once you have them? For example, do they become a part of a mailing list?

- If so, are there specific mailing campaigns which are sent to people depending on how interested they are or how warm they are as a lead?

- If there are mail shot campaigns, are they pre-written or will you have to put them together?

- Are there systems in place to regularly maintain contact with repeat customers?

- Exactly how are these systems organized?

These are important questions because knowing the answers will save you a lot of aggravation in the long run. If the company does not provide this level of support, you can then decide as to whether or not you are prepared to put in the work required to substitute for the lack of clearly defined processes to deal with your leads and customers.

Order Processing

Another aspect of support which can easily be overlooked when doing your research is how easy the order process is. Ease of order processing is a crucial part of the business. You need to be able to easily and quickly process the orders of your customers if you are to make a meaningful income from it. Ask the following questions:

- -Who is responsible for processing customer orders?
- -What exactly is the order process?
- -How much of the order process is handled by the company?
- -How much of the process is automated?
- -What are the shipping fees?

- -Is the distributor responsible for shipping fees or the customer?

Once you have the information, it is another factor to consider when making your decision. Only you know what you are comfortable or not comfortable with when it comes to order handling. If you are expected to take up the responsibility of it, find out what training, if any is provided to ensure that order processing is as smooth as possible for you and your customers.

Chapter 8: Finding the right Team

Humans are social animals and as such, we often do better in teams. Have you ever heard the saying, "Teamwork makes the dream work?" It could not be truer of network marketing. Teamwork involves working together with a group of individuals towards a common goal. It is the ability to direct individual efforts toward the overall aims and objectives of the organization.

Teams which are the most successful, usually consist of people who are selfless and giving, rather than egotistical and selfish. Teams which are full of people who do not want to share their methods for success for the fear of being outperformed are often the least successful and should be avoided. By working together as a team, you maximize your effectiveness as individuals, becoming a stronger force than you would alone. This is because the combined efforts give people the opportunity to operate at their best because they are under less pressure to be good at things which they consider weaknesses. Good teams get together regularly and have brainstorming sessions to thrash out good ideas.

They support each other and motivate each other for the good of the team. Training, marketing, sponsoring and personal development all take place within the team, so choosing the right one is critical to your success as an individual.

This support is very often over and above what the company provides, but is crucial if you are to be successful as a network marketer.

Factors In Choosing The Right Team

Where is the Team Located?

Different companies and teams operate in different ways. For instance, you may find that some companies organise their teams on a regional basis. This means that your team is allocated depending on your location. This can be a good thing or a bad thing. If you like your team, then it is convenient because assuming that it is a "good team" as defined here, you will be able to get to team meetings without too much trouble. Being located physically in the same geographical region is also an advantage if you sell physical products. If you sell physical products and your team is spread all over the country and you need to get to team meetings on a regular basis, then it is probably not a good team to join. On the other hand, if the company you want to join sells virtual products or services which are marketed purely online, the team location is irrelevant. They could be on all four corners of the globe as long as all team members have full access to the internet.

Standardised Marketing Systems

There are some sponsors who insist on using a standardised marketing system and even insist that all members of their team duplicate it. For some sponsors, it is their way or the high way! This is not the kind of team you want to be on. The purpose of the sponsor is to guide you, not to bully you into following his way only. You should be free to use your brain, after all, this is a business opportunity, not a boarding school! Find out in depth details about your sponsors management style by asking the team members.

Team Spirit

Spend a little time with the team members and you will get a sense of whether or not they are excited and passionate about their team and what they are selling. I have said it before and I will say it again, ENTHUSIASM SELLS! There is nothing better in network marketing than being a part of a team of fun people who are passionate about what they are doing. Passion and enthusiasm is contagious and it is transmitted like a virus from person to person. You will pick it up very easily and this will give you a clear indication of how successful the team is and how successful you could be if you are a part of it. In addition to this, you should be able to get a clear idea of the atmosphere within the team. Find out the following by asking some questions.

- Do the team members get along?

- Are there little cliques and gangs within the team?

- Does the team openly share ideas with each other?

- Do they celebrate each other's successes and lift each other up?

Your Sponsor

As previously discussed, you will likely be spending a lot of time working with your sponsor so it is important that you like him as a person! In addition to this, your sponsor must have good leadership qualities. The best leaders lead by action, not with fluffy words. You need to know if their personality and leadership style will work with you as a person. If they are autocratic by nature and you are more of a laid-back kind of person, the relationship probably won't work.

You can easily find out about their personal leadership style by asking the right questions about them and their other team members. Find out if they are the kind of sponsor who will support you constantly in the long-term, or if they are likely to just leave you on your own once you have signed up under them.

Finding the Right Team Leader or Sponsor

Once you have chosen the company you want to join, how you find your team leader depends for starter on whether you need to be geographically near them. If you do, you should start by contacting the company and asking for a list of sponsors in your area. Once you have the list, make the initial contact with the closest ones to you by phone or email and arrange to talk to them in person or through the phone. You should get a good sense of them and their team after spending some time listening to them and asking the questions discussed here.

If your geographic location is irrelevant, again, contact the company and ask for a list of sponsors and take it from there. In addition to everything discussed already, look for the following when you talk to your potential sponsors:

- A sponsor who has experienced the ups and downs of the MLM business is likely to be a good bet. This is because you can learn a lot from them and they are likely to stay the course with you.

- Someone who studies and researches the industry on a regular basis is essential because they will be up-to-date on all the latest marketing methods which they can share with you.

- A leader who subscribes to industry magazines and constantly attends seminars to continuously develop themselves and their team is likely to be a good sponsor.

- They should have a proven track record which you can check up on.

- A good team leader will have realistic goals for himself and his teams because he will constantly be looking at the bigger picture.

- He should be very knowledgeable about marketing. Do a little bit of research and ask him some questions to test his knowledge.

- He should be up-to-date on all things marketing including teleconferencing, direct mail, and internet marketing and social media.

Marketing Materials And Organized Support

Find out if the team has organised an exclusive team training events and webinars. Things to look out for include the following:

- Are there team training calls?

- Are there team webinars?

- Are there any personal development training events for the team?

- Is there help with how to use company marketing tools or third party tools?

- Is there help with three-way calls?

- Is the marketing material provided by your sponsor? and how much does it cost?

- What marketing support or training is provided within the team?

Chapter 9: Final Thoughts

It is important to remember that how good or bad a network marketing company is subjective and depends on your unique needs as an individual. Now that you have all the information, your gut will tell you what is the most important thing for you. For example, the marketability of the product may be the single most important thing for me in terms of whether I decide to join a company or not. But for you, the most important thing may be the superior quality of the product. On the other hand, you may get excited by selling skin care products and I may get excited by selling nutritional products.

Perfection Does Not Exist

Every company in the world will have its good points and bad points. Just like people, the reality is that there is no such thing as a perfect company. There is no point in searching for one because you will never find one. The plus side is that with the knowledge that you have gained from this book, you can find a company that is perfect for you as an individual. This is the reason why this book does not contain endless lists of "good" and "bad" companies! Now that you have all the information required in helping you to effectively evaluate companies, you can make the best decision for YOU.

Research

Adequately researching your opportunities before you jump in is crucial and is ultimately, your responsibility. As is deciding on which of the factors presented to you in this book is most important. Too many people do not take the time to properly research which company is best for them and end up jumping from company to company because something does not feel right or sit right with them. This is a complete waste of valuable time and money. Everybody knows that time is money and every time you join a new opportunity, there is a cost involved. Moving from company to company is not an efficient thing to do and is counterproductive. Therefore, carrying out your research is so important. Now that you know how, go ahead and do it. Don't just put this book down and forget about it! Keep referring to it if you get stuck and be thorough in your investigations if you are serious about creating a sustainable income with network marketing. Despite what the sceptics say, it is entirely possible if you take it seriously.

Check Yourself

Consider using a trusted friend as a sounding board to check your gut instinct and any facts that you have collected. Thoroughly check over the compensation plan and ensure that you are 100% certain that what they claim regarding income potential is in fact, true. Thoroughly check over the terms and conditions before you sign anything. If you can get a free legal advice regarding the terms and conditions, go for it, especially if that will make you feel more comfortable.

Take Your Time

Take your time when making the final decision. Don't feel pressured in signing up to anything or handing money over at opportunity events and meetings. Do not be fooled by anyone telling you things like, "this is a limited time offer!" Speak to other distributors in settings where you feel at ease and can really take your time to ask questions and absorb everything. Whether you are talking to potential team members or sponsors, go with a list of prepared questions, many of which you can copy from this book. This will ensure that confusion does not set in! There is potentially a lot of information to absorb. Be kind to yourself and take some notes to help you keep track of everything. A confused, indecisive mind is not helpful.

Be Yourself

Consider if the plan you are looking into is suitable to your particular talents, interests and goals. Remember that network marketing money does not come from magic. It takes hard work to build up a client base and a downline. When you speak to other distributors, find out how much time they spent getting everything set up from the beginning and ask them how that compares to the time they spend on the business now. Compare that information to the expectations you have and the level of commitment you are prepared to give.

Final Warnings

I would never tell you NOT to join a company or not to take advantage of an exciting opportunity, but below are three red flags you should be aware of. Be extra vigilant and do extra research before diving into any of the following:

1. Start-ups: Every year, thousands of brands new MLM companies start up with promises of spectacular sales and enticing income streams. The fact is that most of these companies FAIL within one year or are just actually starting up. I am not saying that there are not some unique and special start-ups out there with the potential to be successful companies. I am simply saying that a start-up is a risk. By joining a start-up, you risk your time, your hard work, your money and the loss of potential income you could have earned elsewhere. Be vigilant and do a bit of extra digging into start-ups before you jump in at the deep-end and take a risk.

2. Limited Market Products: Limited market products are simply products which are aimed at a segment of the population. It could be a niche product or it could be something aimed specifically at women, men, children, women of a certain age... You get the picture. While being limited to a market is not necessarily a kiss of death, it is definitely something to consider when doing your research. However, most companies are smart enough to diversify their product range, just in case. If you find yourself looking at a company who specifically targets a limited market, beware!

3. Fad Products: Do you remember the laundry ball? It was a small plastic ball that you put into the tumble dryer which supposedly help your clothes dry faster and be fluffier (I talked about it in the products chapter). That company did not stick around very long and I am sure you can imagine what happened to the pay checks of those who were distributing those balls. Some products are just not viable for long-term and it is easy to spot fad products most of the time. Some technological products also naturally fall into this category simply because of the speed at which technology moves in terms of innovation. As discussed in the chapter on investigating the industry, unless the technology product is one of a diverse range of consumable technology products, it is best to steer clear.

Considerations

In closing, with network marketing, you can start a profitable, legitimate business for as little as $100. Furthermore, you can even choose the person who is going to coach you to success. The difference between a competent network marketer who fails and one who succeeds is simple. Those who have the foresight to choose:

1. The most suitable industry for them.

2. The most suitable company and products for them.

3. The best sponsor for them.

4. The best team for them.

All four of those choices have one thing in common, they all relate to you choosing the best thing for you as an individual. Remember, right at the start, we said that there was no such thing as the best company, only the best company for you. Remember that a good sponsor is a vital ingredient! All successful business people and athletes have good sponsors, mentors and coaches behind them giving them the benefit of their insight and experience. Make sure that you give yourself the best chance by choosing the best possible person for you.

GOOD LUCK!

If you liked the book and gained some knowledge that will be useful to you in life, then please leave an honest review to help others find this book. It will be a small effort on your part, but an act of charity that may help in changing few lives for the better. We thank you in advance for your help.

This book is about fundamental principles of wealth creation that can be applied to any business or investing strategy. At Wealth Creation Academy, we teach multitude ways to generate passive income, which includes: real estate investing, digital publishing, affiliate marketing, multi-level marketing and investing in forex, commodities, and shares by copying experienced traders that need very little of time. You may like to get started with some of the strategies depending on your budget and time.

Other Books by the Authors

Praveen Kumar has authored several bestselling books. Please visit his website **http://praveenkumarauthor.com/** for more information

About the Authors

Praveen Kumar was abandoned by his father at the age of fourteen and joined the Navy at tender age of fifteen where education, roof and free food were guaranteed.

In order to understand the root cause of suffering he turned towards philosophy and religion. After 10 years of soul searching and meditation he understood that 'life is 'and material and spiritual world are closely interwoven. You cannot live in one without the other.

Praveen was highly successful in the Navy, where he successfully commanded submarines, sailed around the world in a yacht and received gallantry award for his contribution to the Navy.

Despite his success in the Navy, Praveen realized that lack of financial security for his family was one of key root causes of his suffering, resulting from his childhood deprivation. To improve his financial standing, Praveen took pre-mature retirement from the Navy to build his financial future through investing in Real Estate. The decision to educate on financial matters paid off, and today he and his wife are comfortably retired on six-figure passive income.

His aim is to help others create wealth in an enlightened way and empower them to live a healthy and happy life. He dedicates his time to write books and articles on financial and spiritual matters.

Prashant graduated with distinction from Auckland University as a computer engineer and later completed his MBA from the world's leading institution - INSEAD. During his successful corporate career, he worked for the most reputable consulting firms in the world - BCG & Deloitte - and represented New Zealand on Prime

Minister-led trade missions to South East Asian countries.

After successfully generating income through his passive investments in property and stocks, Prashant decided to team up with his father to help people transform their lives through the leverage of financial education.

Their website http://wealth-creation-academy.com/ is devoted to teaching people how to create Multiple Streams of Passive Income through investing in real estate, online marketing and creating digital products